75 LOVE POEMS BOOK 1

FLOWERS

Celebrate Romantic Love

Relatable Poems that You
Will Enjoy

by
Dean S. Harrison

Published by Harrison Global Media, LLC.

Contents

Introduction

In the ever-turning pages of human history, few things have captivated the hearts and minds of men and women as enduringly as love poetry. **75 Love Poems Book 1 Flowers** by Dean S. Harrison stands as a testament to this age-old tradition, weaving together threads of passion, yearning, joy, and sorrow into a rich tapestry of verse. Drawing inspiration from the great romantic poets—whose words have echoed through the corridors of time—this collection invites readers to explore the depths of human emotion and the ineffable mysteries of the heart.

As you immerse yourself in these verses, you will discover that each poem is not just an expression of love, but a key to understanding the complex nature of this most profound human experience.

20 Benefits of Reading **75 Love Poems Book 1 Flowers**:

1. **Enhances Emotional Intelligence**: Romantic poetry helps readers understand and express their emotions more effectively.

2. **Stimulates Creativity**: The metaphorical language of poetry fosters creative thinking and imagination.

3. **Strengthens Empathy**: By connecting with the emotions of others through poetry, readers develop a deeper sense of empathy.

4. **Improves Language Skills**: Engaging with the nuanced language of poetry enhances vocabulary and articulation.

5. **Encourages Self-Reflection**: Poetry prompts introspection about relationships, love, and personal growth.

6. **Provides Solace**: In moments of loneliness or heartache, poetry offers comfort and companionship.

7. **Celebrates Beauty**: Romantic poetry often explores the beauty of both the natural world and human experience.

8. **Fosters Connection**: Sharing and discussing poetry can lead to strengthened relationships with others who have similar interests.

9. **Enhances Memory**: The rhythmic and structured nature of poetry makes it an effective tool for improving memory.

10. **Offers New Perspectives**: Poetry provides insights into different eras, cultures, and personal experiences with love.

11. **Promotes Mindfulness**: The contemplative nature of reading poetry encourages a present, mindful state.

12. **Encourages Critical Thinking**: Analyzing poems develops critical and interpretative skills.

13. **Supports Healing**: Emotional expression through poetry can be therapeutic and healing.

14. **Boosts Cultural Literacy**: Romantic poetry is a key component of literary history and cultural discourse.

15. **Inspires Writing**: Reading poetry can motivate readers to write their own verses and express their feelings creatively.

16. **Provides Historical Insight**: Many poems reflect the social and cultural contexts of their times, offering historical perspectives.

17. **Cultivates Aesthetic Appreciation**: The artful language and form of poetry enhance appreciation for artistic expressions.

18. **Promotes Relaxation**: The rhythm and flow of poetry can have a calming effect, reducing stress.

19. **Enriches the Soul**: Engaging with profound themes in poetry can lead to a deeper, more fulfilling life experience.

20. **Sparks Joy**: The beauty of a perfectly crafted poem can lift spirits and bring joy.

75 Love Poems Book 1 Flowers is more than just a collection; it is a journey through the landscape of the heart. As you delve into these poems, you may find not only beauty and inspiration but also a deeper connection with the world around you and the loved ones with whom you share your life.

Flowers

In our room, flowers frame your gentle grace,
Bright blooms reflect the smile on your face.
Morning beams catch each petal's glow,
In your light, these blossoms grow.

Shadows stretch from the vase to the wall,
Echoing whispers of your soft footfall.
Stems arch toward the light, lean and long,
Drawn, like me, by your siren song.

Your laughter lingers, light and low,
A melody making my love overflow.
The scent of roses, sweet, profound,
Tells of the love that we have found.

In corners quiet of our shared life,
Flowers stand, slicing strife like a knife.
Their transient beauty, brief, sublime,
Mirrors our moments, suspended in time.

Each bloom, each fleeting, fragrant flower,
Marks a minute, a day, a dawning hour.
In this vase, these simple sprays,
Hold the essence of our sunlit days.

Photography

In the mountain woods, ferns unfurl with grace,
You aim your lens, capturing their trace.
Their green fronds fan out, intricate and wild,
Mirroring the laughter of nature's child.

Through your eyes, the forest comes alive,
Each captured image destined to survive.
Your focus sharp, the ferns sway soft,
In the viewfinder, our worlds aloft.

We tread lightly on the forest floor,
Your shutter clicks, each snap implores.
Capturing moments of quiet, of calm,
In the woods, a healing balm.

You find beauty in the details small,
The texture of bark, the leaf's fall.
Your camera, a tool that lets you see,
The hidden wonders that come to be.

Sunlight filters through the trees,
Dances on leaves, a soft tease.
It plays on your face, highlights aglow,
In these woods, love continues to grow.

Each photo a testament, a silent speech,
Of the beauty within our easy reach.
In these moments, as you frame and shoot,
Our love grows roots, our bond takes root.

Lighthouse

By the lighthouse, where the waves crash bold,
We lean and share dreams as the night's air cold.
Your hand in mine, a steady, sure embrace,
As we envision futures, time cannot erase.

The lighthouse stands, a sentinel of light,
Guiding ships through the stormy night.
Like its beam, your love leads me through,
In the darkened world, my beacon's hue.

Waves crash below, a symphony of sound,
In this sacred space, our dreams are bound.
Your eyes, alight with visions so clear,
Reflect the hope that draws us near.

We speak of days when our hair turns grey,
Of love that deepens, come what may.
With each word whispered, future's bright,
Illuminated by the lighthouse light.

The ocean's roar, a backdrop to our plans,
As we stand united, hand in hand.
In the lighthouse's shadow, strong and true,
I see a lifetime to spend with you.

Together we dream of places unseen,
Of sunsets and starlit nights serene.
Your voice, a melody, soft and sweet,
In the future's promise, our hearts meet.

The waves may crash, the winds may wail,
But in your love, I will not fail.
Leaning on the lighthouse, we stand tall,
With you, my love, I have it all.

So let the ocean's tumult rage and roar,
For our love's light will endure evermore.
By the lighthouse, our visions align,
In the crashing waves, your hand in mine.

Hot Air Balloon

In a hot air balloon, we softly sway,
Above the fields and streams, far away.
Your kiss, a touch of heaven's serene,
In the patchwork below, a quilted dream.

The basket holds us, high in the sky,
Where worries wane and whispers fly.
Your lips meet mine, in a tender touch,
A moment of magic, meaning much.

Fields below, a mosaic of green,
Streams winding through, a silver sheen.
Our love floats free, in the open air,
With every kiss, no burden to bear.

The horizon stretches, endless and wide,
In this balloon, with you by my side.
Your smile, a beacon, bright and true,
Guides our journey in skies so blue.

The gentle breeze, a soft caress,
Echoes the joy of our shared success.
In this lofty embrace, love's pure delight,
Kissing you here, everything feels right.

Above the earth, where dreams take flight,
We find our haven, day or night.
Your eyes, a sparkle, stars in the day,
Reflecting love in the light's soft sway.

In the quiet calm of the balloon's glide,
Our hearts beat steady, side by side.
Kissing in the sky, our spirits soar,
In this serene space, I love you more.

So let us float where the world can't see,
In our hot air balloon, just you and me.
For in your kiss, I find my tune,
A love that rises, like a hot air balloon.

Oranges

In the orchard, under the sun's warm gaze,
We reach for oranges, caught in their blaze.
Their rind is rough, the scent bursts free,
As you smile, picking each one for me.

Your hands grasp gently, peel back green leaves,
Revealing fruits born from light's long heaves.
Each orange a sun, small and bright,
Nestled in branches, a delightful sight.

The tree limbs laden, bow with the weight,
Of sun-kissed spheres that for our touch wait.
You hand them down, your laughter rings,
In this simple joy, my heart finds wings.

Your fingers, stained with citrus sweet,
Brush against mine, our eyes meet.
This moment simple, under the orange tree's arm,
Holds a quiet magic, a farmyard charm.

We fill our basket, but more so our day,
With the colors and tastes that in memories stay.
Oranges piled high, their zest in the air,
Around us, a halo, caught in your hair.

Back home, we'll squeeze them, their juice rich and ripe,
But here, in this moment, it's the love that's the type.
To stand here with you, under trees that provide,
Is to know the sweetness that in life, does reside.

Listening to Classical Music

In the hall where violins weep and sigh,
We sit together, you and I.
The orchestra's swell fills the air,
As music lifts the evening's fare.

Strings sing out a tender call,
Echoes dance along the hall.
Each note played, a wordless speech,
A gentle lesson they do teach.

Your hand in mine, under the light,
We lose ourselves in sound tonight.
The melody, like a flowing stream,
Carries us through a waking dream.

Piano keys rise soft and low,
Matching the mood in the ebb and flow.
With each crescendo's powerful rise,
I see the spark within your eyes.

Violins whisper with the breeze,
Notes float softly, hearts to please.
In this symphony's embrace,
Time slows down, suspends its pace.

As the final note gently dies,
A quiet truth in the silence lies.
With music's end, it's clear to see,
Life's sweetest song plays when you're with me.

Sunset

On the shore where the gentle waves do play,
We watch the sunset close the day.
The sky ignites with fiery hues,
Painting our moments in amber clues.

The ocean mirrors the changing sky,
Where orange and pink and purple lie.
Your silhouette against the light,
Holds all the beauty of the night.

Our hands entwine, our hearts connect,
In this twilight, our lives reflect.
The soft sand beneath, the cool air above,
Here on this beach, I whisper my love.

The horizon blends where colors meet,
A canvas vast, a sight so sweet.
Your eyes catch the last of the sun's great fire,
Glowing with untold, deep desire.

As the stars begin to softly appear,
In the dimming light, I hold you near.
The world retreats, the night takes hold,
In your arms, I fend off the cold.

With each wave that laps upon the shore,
My heart, like the tide, longs for more.
Here with you, where the sky meets the sea,
Forever is where I want to be.

Driving by The Cherry Blossom Trees

Beneath the boughs of cherry bloom,
We drive, our hearts in sync, consume.
Petals dance on winds that play,
Fluttering forth in a fragrant ballet.

Down the road where blossoms frame,
Each scene painted with pink acclaim.
Your laughter fills the springtime air,
In this moment, none but you compare.

Cherry petals, soft and light,
Adorn our path, arrest the sight.
They swirl around with graceful ease,
Carried forth by the gentlest breeze.

With each mile under skies so clear,
I find new reasons to hold you dear.
The road unwinds, our journey long,
But in your presence, I belong.

Through tunnels made of blooming trees,
We cruise beneath the floral seas.
The world outside may shift and change,
Yet our love remains, unstrange.

As petals settle on the dash,
Our time together, never brash.
On this road, flanked by spring's own cheer,
I cherish every moment, dear.

With you beside me in the drive,
Every second comes alive.
On this path where beauty resides
Forever feels near, as time abides.

Candle

In twilight's tender, trembling touch,
A candle flickers, fears too much.
Its flame flutters, fragile, faint,
Besieged by breezes, breaths constraint.

Yet in your gaze, so soft, so sure,
The light finds strength, begins to cure.
Your whispers ward the wounding wind,
Within your warmth, the flames befriend.

Beside this beacon, barely bright,
We watch the wax wane in the night.
Yet hope, like our hearts, holds tight,
In dimming depths, it clings to light.

Each gust that gathers, grim and grey,
Seems set to snatch our small spark away.
But steadfast, sure, our love's soft glow,
Guards the gleam against the blow.

Together, through tempests tried and true,
Our bond binds tighter, builds anew.
The candle's courage, caught from you,
Burns bright, belies the breezy rue.

In every storm that strains the wick,
Your love, like light, lays on thick.
And so this candle, by wind kissed,
Stands still, survives, in shadows' midst.

Swimming in the Sea

On summer's stage, the sun sits high,
A blazing beacon in the blue sky.
We wade into the welcoming waves,
Where water whispers and beckons brave.

Hand in hand, we dive deep,
Sea's embrace, in its sweep.
Sunlight scatters through the swell,
A shimmering dance where sea sprites dwell.

Your laughter launches, light and free,
Riding ripples of the radiant sea.
Together tumbling through turquoise tides,
Where warmth and water wondrously collide.

Beneath the surface, silent, serene,
We swim in scenes so surreal, unseen.
Your eyes, emerald, echo the ocean's hue,
A reflection of love, deep and true.

Surfacing, we share salty kisses,
In this seascape of summertime blisses.
Sun-kissed skin, salt-streaked hair,
In this moment, nothing can compare.

As the day declines, the dusk draws near,
Still, in this sea, all I hold dear.
With you, my wife, where waves wash ashore,
I find a love to last, forevermore.

Driving Home

In the night's navy cloak, I navigate alone,
Lost in lanes where light has barely shone.
The twisting turns tell tales unclear,
Each empty echo breeds a breath of fear.

Streetlamps stutter, scarce in their glow,
Casting cryptic shadows on the road below.
I wander, wayward, without a trace,
Seeking signs or sights of a familiar face.

My mind meanders, a maze of doubt,
Each decision driven by routes reroute.
Yet in this darkness, despairing and deep,
A vision of you in my mind does creep.

Guiding gently, your grace appears,
Calming the chaos, quieting fears.
Though roads may wind where wrong turns tempt,
Your love lights my way, a lasting lamp.

Through the thick of night, your heart's my home,
No longer lost, no need to roam.
In dreams you draw near, a beacon bright,
Guiding me gently through the gritty night.

So I'll follow the feeling, the fire you've lit,
Through twisting trails, I'll never quit.
For in the night's embrace, as I yearn and roam,
It's thoughts of you that bring me home.

The Pier

On the pier at night, where whispers wane,
We wander where the waters deign
To mirror moonlight, mellow, mild,
Reflecting ripples, softly styled.

The lamps along the lonely length
Cast golden glows of gentle strength,
Their light on languid waves lay down,
Silver shadows in the sound.

At the pier's end, a peaceful pause,
We stand and savor without cause.
Your arms around me, anchor tight,
In the embrace of evening light.

Beneath the blanket of the night,
The stars above us, sparse but bright,
We breathe the briny breeze that blows,
Sharing secrets only the sea knows.

The world withdraws, the wharf, our stage,
This moment maroons us from the age.
Time turns timid, tides too tame,
In our cocoon where love lays claim.

Here on this haven, hushed and whole,
Heart to heart, soul to soul,
The night enfolds us, endless, deep,
In love's embrace, we softly steep.

On the Highway

As we drive down the coast, the wind weaves through,
Your hair, like waves, in rhythm move.
The sun sets slowly, sending shades,
Painting pictures as daylight fades.

Your tresses toss, a tempest true,
Catching colors of crimson hue.
Softly singing, the radio plays,
A melody that gently sways.

The chords carry, caress the air,
Blending with breezes in your hair.
The windows down, the world just right,
With you beside me in the fading light.

Each strand that swirls, a story spun,
Under the ember end of sun.
The music's whisper, waves' soft call,
At this moment, I have it all.

Your laughter lifts, and lingers long,
A perfect chorus to our song.
As miles stretch out beneath our wheels,
Your beauty, the breeze, it all feels real.

Through turns and tides, your hair flies free,
A dance of joy, of ecstasy.
So let's keep driving, let the night descend,
With music our companion, and love that never ends.

Snow

Beneath a blanket, bound so tight,
We watch the whimsy of winter's white.
Snowflakes fall, so soft, so slow,
A silent dance by the window's glow.

Your warmth wends its way to mine,
In cozy communion, our spirits align.
The world outside wears a wintry shroud,
But here inside, warmth is vowed.

Each flake that floats finds its fate,
A gentle descent, delicate, sedate.
Our breaths blend, a bonded beat,
In rhythms of warmth, so soft, so sweet.

Nestled near, no need for words,
The quiet comfort, like flight of birds,
Glides gracefully, under grey skies,
In the tranquil track where contentment lies.

Outside, the chill may claim its due,
But under this blanket, I'm warmed by you.
Your presence, a harbor, home and hearth,
Against the frost, a fortress of mirth.

Let the snow sweep, let the cold call,
Within these walls, winter seems small.
For wrapped in warmth, with you beside,
The storm's a show, nothing to hide.

Eyes

In the sparkle of your eyes, stories play,
Each word a weave in the web of our day.
As you recount with a radiant smile,
Every moment, every mundane mile.

The gleam that grows with each tale told,
Bright as the sun, yet gentle as gold.
Each thread you spin, so precious, so pure,
Weaves a tapestry that will endure.

In the luster of your laughter, life is light,
Tales of the day turn darkness bright.
Your voice, a velvet vibrant thread,
Colors the canvas of the path we tread.

With each narrative, your eyes ignite,
Shimmering windows reflecting light.
A glance, a giggle, grace intertwined,
In the stories shared, our souls find.

Your excitement echoes in eloquent eyes,
Each blink, a brushstroke in our skies.
The stories you sew, stitch by stitch,
Bind us, build us, without a hitch.

As night nears and tales taper to close,
Your eyes still sparkle, your cheer still shows.
In the glow of your gaze, I see my mate,
In each word, the warp and weft of fate.

Evening

As evening descends, the dusk delicately drawn,
We stroll through the city as day is withdrawn.
Your head on my shoulder, so softly it lies,
Beneath the broad blanket of indigo skies.

The twinkling lights trace our tranquil trail,
A path paved in starlight, in the streetlamp's pale.
Around us, the city sings a subdued song,
A melody of moments where hearts belong.

Your breath, a whisper against my skin,
A subtle sign of the serenity within.
Our steps synchronize in silent accord,
In each shared stride, our spirits restored.

The city's heartbeat, hushed and low,
Sets the scene in its gentle glow.
Your presence, a peaceful, perfect weight,
Balances the burdens, undoes the late.

Under these lights, love lightly treads,
Casting shadows, weaving threads.
With your head on my shoulder, the world seems right,
Our love the lighthouse in the looming night.

Each heartbeat under your head, a hymn,
In the cathedral of night, where lights grow dim.
This quiet walk, a waltz, a whispered art,
With you here on my shoulder, hand on my heart.

Sunday

On a lazy Sunday, sunlight streams,
As we linger over brunch, lost in dreams.
Laughter lilts through the air, light and free,
From old jokes that jog sweet memory.

Eggs and echoes of laughter blend,
In the quiet corners of time we spend.
Coffee cups clink, a casual choir,
As past punchlines fuel the fire.

Each chuckle shared, a cherished link,
In the laughter's lilt, our lives sync.
Your smile spreads across your face,
Filling our kitchen with warmth and grace.

Syrup sweet on pancakes poured,
Like the memories across the table stored.
Each sip of coffee, each shared glance,
Strengthens the stitches of our romance.

The morning wanes, our laughter lingers,
Savored by time's gentle fingers.
In jokes retold, in tales re-spun,
Our hearts hold tight to the fun.

A lazy brunch, a simple scene,
Rich with the residue of places we've been.
Here with you, the world feels right,
Wrapped in laughter's loving light.

Thunder Storm

In the storm's embrace, where thunder roars,
We find our refuge, indoors.
Holding you close as the heavens cry,
The rain's rhythm beats a lullaby.

Against the window, raindrops race,
Their drumming hearts keep a frantic pace.
Yet here within, the world stands still,
In our embrace, a tranquil thrill.

The lightning's lace in the night sky drawn,
A flash that fades before the dawn.
But in my arms, you're safe and sound,
Where love's strength is tightly bound.

Your heartbeat hums along with mine,
In sync with the storm's serenade divine.
Thunder rumbles, a distant drum,
Under its beat, our hearts become one.

The storm outside may rage and roar,
Yet every drop sounds like a score.
A melody of might and mist,
In your arms, by love kissed.

As the tempest turns the night,
Our clasped hands hold each other tight.
With you, the storm I dare defy,
In our sheltered sigh, the storm's just shy.

So let the rain recount our love,
Echoing what we're speaking of.
In this storm, safely stored,
Together, our love's chords restored.

In a Crowded Room

In a room where voices vie and merge,
Your hand finds mine, an electric surge.
A silent promise softly pressed,
In that touch, my soul feels blessed.

Amid the clamor, chaos reigns,
Yet your grasp grounds, sustains.
A simple gesture, small but sure,
Speaks of love that will endure.

Through the throng, our fingers thread,
A whispered pact, no words said.
Your warmth wends its way to my wrist,
In that hold, our hearts exist.

As chatter charts around us spin,
Our quiet bond becomes our kin.
The noise may swell, the night grow deep,
Yet in your grip, my fears sleep.

A touch that tells of steady stars,
Unseen but known, from afar.
Among the many, we are two,
Connected, constant, tried and true.

In that crowded space, a world apart,
We stand, hand to heart.
The room may buzz, may burst, may swirl,
Yet in your hand, I find my world.

Your fingers folding into mine,
A fortress formed, no need to pine.
In that clasp, a comfort known,
Together, though the crowd has grown.

Garden

In the garden's glow, where sunlight slips,
My love bends low, with dirt-dabbed lips.
Her hands hold earth, her focus found,
Among the blooms that bound the ground.

Sunlight sifts through leaves above,
Dappling her devotion with beams of love.
Each plant placed with perfect care,
In the soil's embrace, her solace·there.

Her concentration, a canvas clear,
Where nature whispers, close and near.
With every tender touch, she tends,
A tapestry of life she mends.

Her brow is furrowed, thoughtful, deep,
In her garden's keep, her secrets seep.
The world withdraws, its worries wane,
In her realm of root and rain.

Leaves rustle with a rhythmic rust,
Her dedication, a quiet thrust.
This hallowed ground where time is tamed,
By the gardener's grace, her peace proclaimed.

The dance of light through each green leaf,
Highlights her heart, her belief.
In this garden, love and life align,
In every curve, her care's design.

As she nurtures nature's draw,
In awe I watch, in love I thaw.
Here in the garden, under sun's soft sieve,
I see the love she's born to give.

Stealing Kisses

In the kitchen's quiet clasp, where whispers wait,
We steal a kiss as the kettle contemplates.
In mundane moments, magic made,
Turning tasks to tender escapades.

Beneath the buzzing boil's begin,
Our lips meet quick, a grin within.
The steam stirs softly, rising, reeling,
Matching the warmth that we are feeling.

A gentle peck while pasta pours,
Another as the sauce endures.
Each sip of time, a secret shared,
In cooking chores, our love declared.

The hum of home in background beat,
Yet in your arms, my heart's retreat.
We dance between the pots and pans,
A choreography that love commands.

With every task, a touch, a tease,
Simple joys that always please.
The kettle calls with rising steam,
Yet in your kiss, I'm lost in dream.

Turning moments into mirth,
Finding bliss in the daily earth.
As we wait for water's roar,
Love finds a way to mean much more.

In every small, shared slice of day,
Your love lights paths in soft display.
Waiting on the kettle's tune,
Our kitchen dances, afternoon.

The Fireplace

By the flickering fire's friendly glow,
She reads in rhythm soft and slow.
Pages turn in tender trace,
Yet she reaches out, our fingers lace.

Absorbed in tales as flames dance high,
Her silent laughter, softest sigh.
The firelight flutters on her face,
In this quiet, quaint and cozy place.

Her world within the written word,
Yet her heart's beat still is heard.
She finds my hand without a look,
A gentle gesture, no need for hook.

Lost in lore, yet linked by touch,
This simple act means just so much.
The warmth from the hearth, the warmth of her skin,
Melds magic moments where dreams begin.

The crackling comfort, the stories' call,
In this shared silence, we have it all.
Her presence, a peaceful, potent balm,
Her touch, a tether, in evening's calm.

By the glowing grate we sit and stay,
Hours dissolve, night eats the day.
Each chapter's close, her eyes meet mine,
In the fire's fade, our lives entwine.

In this room, the world feels right,
With my love lost in literary light.
By the fire, where embers burn,
She gifts me moments, page by turn.

Joy

In the park where playful whispers weave,
Her laughter lifts on the springtime breeze.
With our children, she chases, cheers, and charms,
Her happiness holds them in her arms.

Her joy jumps higher than the swings can swing,
Brighter than the blooms that bloom in spring.
In her eyes, a sparkle, a special spark,
Igniting imaginations in the park.

Her mirth, a melody that mingles with air,
Sweeter than the scents that swirl without care.
The slide's descent, the seesaw's sway,
Her delight dances in the day.

Round the merry-go-round, with glee she glides,
In every game, her spirit presides.
Her laughter, a leader, light and free,
Casting spells of bliss on bended knee.

The sandbox, a stage for her joyful jest,
Building castles, crafting quests.
Her voice vaults, vibrant under the sky,
As kites with our kids courageously fly.

In this field of freedom, her fondness flows,
Like the wind that whispers and gently blows.
With each laugh shared in the sun's embrace,
Our family finds a perfect place.

So here in the park, her joy's refrain,
Turns mundane moments to magic, plain.
Her laughter, a gift that lifts and gives,
In her joy, our sweet life lives.

Coffee

In the morning's murmur, mugs meet,
Across the table, our eyes greet.
With every sip, a silent say,
In shared glances to start the day.

Her smile sends sweetness through the steam,
A quiet glow, a gentle gleam.
Coffee cups cradle our calm repose,
As the new day softly, slowly grows.

In these moments, minor and meek,
A language of love, no need to speak.
Her gaze gives grace, a gift to start,
Fuel not just for day, but for heart.

Under the aroma, rich and deep,
Promises we silently keep.
The warmth from the cup, the warmth in her look,
A perfect page in our life's book.

Each morning meeting, our ritual, our rite,
Where love's language is soft and light.
Her eyes hold stories, simple, serene,
In the quiet coffee scene.

Our cups clink, a casual chime,
In rhythm with our routine time.
This daily dance, delicate and dear,
Marks each morning we hold near.

Through coffee steam, her spirit shines,
In these small sips, her heart aligns.
With every glance, a sweet embrace,
In the morning's mild, we find our grace.

Christmas

In our home, her hands work wonders wide,
As holidays approach with a festive tide.
With each adornment, each garland's grace,
She crafts a corner, a cherished space.

Her touch transforms the everyday,
Into scenes of joy, where bright colors play.
Garlands glimmer along the stair,
Her creativity cast everywhere.

Ribbons wrap 'round rails, resplendent, rich,
Tapestries tell tales in every niche.
The sparkle of lights, strung with care,
Dance in her eyes, delight in her air.

Ornaments, old and new, nestle and hang,
Echoing softly the songs we once sang.
Under her guidance, the tree stands tall,
Decked in delights, delighting us all.

Candles catch the calm, crisp night,
Casting shadows soft, a sight so bright.
Her laughter layers the festive air,
Filling our home with flair beyond compare.

In every corner, a touch of her art,
Her festive spirit, a vital part.
With tinsel and twine, traditions twirl,
Around my heart, my festive girl.

Through her eyes, the holidays unfold,
A tapestry of time, treasured and told.
In our home, where her heart lays the scene,
Her creativity kindles a holiday dream.

Journal

In the quiet corners of morning's muse,
She writes her whispers, the words she chooses.
Her journal, a journey through thoughts deep,
Where secrets of her soul safely sleep.

Each entry etched with earnest care,
Expressions of love she longs to share.
Her pen, poised to portray her heart,
Crafts sentences that are works of art.

Lines lay bare the depth of her desire,
Ink ignites like sparks from fire.
Her thoughts thread through each tender page,
Revealing the richness of her sage.

With each word woven, wisdom shown,
In prose that proves her love has grown.
Her sentences, a soft sonnet's flow,
In the quiet glow of lamp's low throw.

Her journal holds her heart's true weight,
With love inscribed by hands of fate.
Her musings mirror the mind's deep caves,
In scripted signs of waves and graves.

This book, a binding of her being's breadth,
Holds more than words—it holds her breath.
In pages pressed with love's own print,
Her heart and soul are subtly hint.

In every line, her love declared,
In every word, her soul bared.
Through her journal, I journey too,
To the heart of the woman I thought I knew.

Traveling

On long drives, the road rolls beneath,
Her hand rests gently, a soothing sheath.
The miles stretch out, endless and wide,
In her presence, peace does abide.

Her touch, a token of tender grace,
Brings calm to the cabin, our enclosed space.
The landscape changes, hills give way to plains,
Yet her comfort constant, ever remains.

Through winding ways and stretching streets,
Her serene smile, my heart greets.
Her laughter lightens the lengthy ride,
With her here, joy joins my side.

The hum of the highway, our steady song,
With her hand in mine, nothing feels wrong.
The world outside might rush and roar,
But inside, her calm creates more.

Under the vastness of the vaulted sky,
Her eyes explore as we pass by.
Her presence, a pulse of potent peace,
Makes each mile less of a lease.

As dusk descends and headlights glow,
Her warmth weaves wonders I've come to know.
With her beside me, the road less daunting,
Our shared silence, softly haunting.

Every journey, every long drive,
Her love, the reason I thrive.
With her hand on my knee, the road ahead clear,
In every moment, I hold her dear.

Silhouette

Her silhouette, a soft shape against the sunset's blaze,
Stands steadfast, gazing at the ocean's vast maze.
The sky bleeds colors, crimson and gold,
Her form framed in the fire, bold and bold.

She watches waves, their endless ebb and flow,
Her thoughts whispering soft, a gentle, tidal tow.
The sun sinks slowly, swallowed by the sea,
Her profile painted in the light's final plea.

Against the amber air, her outline etched,
A picture of peace, perfectly sketched.
The sea's soft song sings in sync with her soul,
In this moment, the world seems whole.

Her eyes explore the horizon's fading line,
Seeking secrets in the saline brine.
The ocean's breath, a background hum,
To the quiet cadence of the life we've come.

Each wave's retreat, a tug at her heart,
Her gaze glued to the place where sky and water part.
This twilight tapestry, a backdrop vast,
Captures her calm, her peace to last.

In the sunset's surrender, she finds her muse,
Her silhouette softens, hues infuse.
With her there, the ocean not just a view,
But a mirror reflecting her, deep and true.

So stands my love, silhouette aglow,
A part of the panorama, the evening's show.
Her presence paints my sunset sky,
A perfect scene as night draws nigh.

The Grove

In a secluded grove, where whispers weave,
Your name floats forth from the autumn leaves.
The trees stand tall, their secrets keep,
Where once we carved initials deep.

Each breeze that brushes through the boughs,
Carries the cadence of our vows.
Your name, a soft, sustained song,
In this grove where shadows belong.

Leaves rustle with the resonance of your voice,
In the hush of the grove, my heart rejoices.
The sunlight slips through each slender seam,
Casting patterns where our past might seem.

Amidst the arms of ancient trees,
Your name rides the restless breeze.
It dances, delicate, a dulcet tone,
In the grove where I'm never alone.

The bark bears the badges of our love,
Carved carefully in the canopy above.
Our initials intertwined, forever to stay,
As seasons shift, in night and day.

This sacred space, our secret shared,
Where whispered winds show how much I cared.
Your name, a mantra, mild and meek,
In the grove where the leaves speak.

With each visit, a visceral thrill,
Here, time tapers, seems to still.
Your essence echoes, an eternal embrace,
In this grove, our special place.

Dinner

In candlelight's caress, your features find their form,
Soft shadows dance across your face, so warm.
The flickering flame frames your serene sight,
Illuminating our intimate night.

Your eyes echo the ember's gentle glow,
Holding secrets only the heart can know.
Each glance glimmers with a gracious glee,
Revealing the depth of your soul to me.

Our table set for two, a tender scene,
Silver and crystal under light so keen.
Your smile, a soft spectacle to behold,
More precious to me than silver or gold.

With every candle flick, your beauty burns brighter,
In this shared silence, our bond grows tighter.
The world wanes away in the wax's slow melt,
Leaving just us, and the emotions we've felt.

Your laughter, a light lyrical lift,
Drifts across the table, a perfect gift.
The candle's glow, golden and giving,
Shadows our supper, shapes our living.

As we dine, the candle dwindles down,
But in its light, love's lure is found.
For in this glow, no words need speak,
The flame flickers, and my heart leaps.

So here, by candlelight, let time delay,
Your illuminated beauty takes my breath away.
In this quiet corner, with you, my dear,
Every moment cherished, every smile sincere.

The Vineyard

In the vineyard's vast, verdant view,
Your laughter leaps, a lively clue.
Between the rows of ripening grapes,
Our joy unfurls, in playful shapes.

Your giggles glide through the green,
Echoing where our feet have been.
Chasing shadows, chasing light,
We romp beneath the sun so bright.

Your smile sparks the sweetest wine,
From every grape on every vine.
Through leaves and vines, our laughter weaves,
A tapebuilder of moments the heart believes.

Around us, the air alive with zest,
Matches the mirth in your chest.
Your eyes alight with amorous fire,
Fuel my fervor, my desire.

Down each row, our footsteps race,
In this lush, leafy embrace.
The vines witness to our whispered jests,
In their boughs, our bond rests.

With every burst of laughter shared,
My soul's soothed, my heart repaired.
You are the melody in the vineyard's song,
With you by my side, I belong.

So let's keep running, love, let's not stop,
Through rows rich with nature's crop.
For in this space, so wide and free,
Your laughter is all I need to be.

Fireworks

On New Year's Eve, beneath the burst of light,
Your eyes catch firework's flight, a splendid sight.
The colors cascade, a vibrant veil,
Reflected in your gaze, where wonders never fail.

Our hands are clasped, a covenant so tight,
Amidst the echoes of the festive night.
Each explosion paints anew above,
While I lose myself in the depths of your love.

Reds and golds glow soft upon your skin,
A tapestry of light, from without and within.
Your face framed by the night's embrace,
Holds all the beauty of the starry space.

As rockets write their brief, bright prose,
Your presence calms, my heartbeat slows.
In your eyes, the night's magic mirrors,
Reflecting moments, magnifying our years.

Together we stand, the old year fades,
Bound by the promise as midnight invades.
Your eyes—a celebration, a sparkling display,
Outshining the fireworks that herald the day.

Let the world around us roar and rise,
I find a universe in your eyes.
With hands held firm and futures bright,
We step together into the night.

On the Train

As the train trails through the misty maze,
You rest against me in a gentle gaze.
Outside, the world whisks by, a whispered blur,
Inside, I kiss your forehead, feelings stir.

Through window's watch, the landscapes merge,
Mountains, meadows, merge to surge.
Yet all the moving, misty scenes,
Can't match the peace your presence means.

Your head on my shoulder, softly lies,
Under the hum of steel, beneath the skies.
I feel your breath, a rhythmic rise,
Matching the train's track, the world's disguise.

My lips meet your forehead in a quiet kiss,
A simple seal of deep, divine bliss.
The mist outside masks our moving train,
But here, in warmth, we remain.

Each mile we pass, each hill we see,
Adds to the story of you and me.
The rhythm of rails, a lulling beat,
In this shared seat, our retreat.

As landscapes slip into foggy folds,
My love for you, deeply holds.
This journey long, through mist and time,
Is sweetened by your touch, sublime.

So let the world blur, let it spin,
With you by my side, I always win.
This gentle journey, where love abides,
Is perfect with you, here by my sides.

On the Hammock at Night

Beneath a blanket of twinkling twilight,
We sway in a hammock, held by the night.
Stars sprinkle the sky, a splendid sight,
As we whisper wishes in the waning light.

The canopy cosmos, vast and deep,
Cradles our conversations, before sleep.
Our hammock hangs, in harmony sways,
Synced with the stars, in celestial plays.

The gentle rock, a rhythmic grace,
In this quiet corner, our peaceful place.
Each star a story, each glow a guide,
With you by my side, in stride we ride.

The universe above, unending, wide,
Mirrors the depth of love inside.
Your laughter lilts, a lovely line,
In the fabric of this night divine.

Nestled close, in nocturnal nest,
In our shared swing, supremely blessed.
The heavens hold our hopes so high,
In the sway of the hammock, under the sky.

Your hand in mine, a perfect fit,
In this starlit sanctuary, we sit.
Here, in the hush of the hovering air,
I find my solace, solace rare.

So let the world whirl, let it spin,
In our hammock haven, we'll always win.
Bound by the beauty of the night,
In this starry silence, our love takes flight.

At the Market

In the bustling heart of the winter market,
We share a scarf, our warmth a compact bracket.
Around us, laughter layers the frosty air,
As festive lights flicker, fair and fair.

Your cheeks are kissed by the cold's crisp bite,
Yet your smile shines, so soft, so bright.
Our breaths billow in blended plumes,
As we wander past wooden booths of blooms.

Through scents of cinnamon, cedar swung,
Around our shared scarf, snugly slung.
Every step syncs, our shoulders brush,
In the crowded cheer, a quiet hush.

The scarf, a silken thread that binds,
Holds us close, its fabric finds.
Woven warmth against winter's chill,
In its embrace, time seems to still.

Hot cocoa clasped in our free hands,
We navigate the night's demands.
The market's magic, merry and bright,
Matches the mirth in your eyes tonight.

With you, the winter's bite turns sweet,
Each market moment, a treat to repeat.
Beneath our scarf, where whispers weave,
I promise to stay, never to leave.

In this shared warmth, the world feels right,
Wrapped up with you on this starlit night.
Our love, like the scarf, a loop without end,
In the weave of winter, you're my warmth, my friend.

On the Porch Swing

On our porch swing, we sit side by side,
Your fingers trace tales where secrets abide.
In the lines of my palm, your touch tends to play,
As the world whirls beyond, in the wane of the day.

The gentle gesture, a soft silent speech,
In the curves of my hand, your caresses reach.
Patterns penned in the palms' pressing parts,
Like whispers woven from the world's heart.

As leaves rustle and the cool breeze blows,
Your touch tells more than anyone knows.
The swing sways in sync with our serene sighs,
Under the umbrella of a slowly fading sky.

Your fingers dance, delicate, defined,
Mapping moments, our memories entwined.
In each motion, a message, a murmured word,
In the language of silence, profoundly heard.

The world passes, people and cars,
Under the watchful eyes of winking stars.
Yet here in our haven, on this humble swing,
Time halts for us, and stillness clings.

With each traced line, a treasure, a token,
Of love spoken in gestures, not just words spoken.
Your touch, a testament to time and tide,
On this porch where peace and patience reside.

In the patterns of your touch, life's lace lies,
A simple pleasure that money can't buy.
Together on this swing, as day dips to night,
In your gentle touch, I find delight.

Dance

In our living room, the world fades away,
As we dance to silence, sway by sway.
Your hair brushes my cheek, a soft caress,
In these quiet moments, our love we confess.

No music plays, yet rhythm finds,
In the heartbeat matching, mind to mind.
Each step we take, a silent song,
In your arms is where I belong.

The gentle graze of your golden strands,
As we twirl and turn, with no demands.
A dance of whispers, tender, true,
In the hush of our haven, just us two.

Your eyes lock mine in a loving leer,
Each glance a gift, crystal clear.
The world outside might rush and roar,
But here inside, time gently soars.

Your touch, a trace, so tender felt,
In the warmth of our embrace, I melt.
The dance floor here, our carpet's embrace,
Turns to a palace in our small space.

No need for music, no need for light,
Your presence alone makes the room bright.
As we glide in grace, in sync we move,
In every step, our love we prove.

So let the silence sing its tune,
Our dance by the dusk, by the rising moon.
With your hair 'gainst my cheek, softly swept,
In your arms, my heart has leapt.

Dusk

In our backyard, as the day descends,
Your sigh spreads serenity, where silence bends.
The sky, a canvas, colors caught aflame,
In your gaze, a golden glow the same.

Your contented exhale, a calming chord,
Plays peacefully as the palette is poured.
Crimson, cerulean, cast across the cloud,
Each hue hums heartily, soft yet proud.

As you lean close, the world wanes away,
Our private viewing of the ending day.
The sun sets slowly, slipping into sleep,
In your sigh, secrets the heavens keep.

Your breath, a breeze beneath the broad expanse,
Adds a rhythm to the night's romance.
Orange and ochre overlay the scene,
Mirroring the warmth in your eyes, serene.

Together we trace the twilight's taper,
No need for words, the sky's paper
Speaks in strokes of splendor spread wide,
With you by my side, in this quiet collide.

Each sigh you send, a whispering wave,
An echo of the ease and peace you crave.
As night nestles neatly in nature's nest,
In your nearness, I find my rest.

Watching the world in its wondrous way,
Your sigh says more than words could say.
In this simple scene, our souls align,
Under the sunset, your hand in mine.

Laughter

By the riverside, we lay our blanket down,
Your smile shines, chasing any frown.
The water whispers, winding its way,
As we steal a slice of the soft-spoken day.

Your laughter launches, light and free,
Lifting the leaves on each leaning tree.
With sandwiches spread and apples to bite,
The day dims down but your delight is bright.

Grasses glisten, green and grand,
Beneath the blue, by the river's hand.
Your eyes, effervescent, echo the sky,
In this tranquil spot where waters lie.

Cheese and crackers neatly packed,
In our little nook, nothing lacked.
With each joke, each giggle you gift,
My spirits soar, suddenly shift.

The river rolls on, a rhythmic route,
Mimicking the melody of your merry shout.
Clouds can't cover the charm you cast,
In the glow of your glee, the grey can't last.

You pick a daisy, place it in your hair,
Beauty so simple, spontaneously spare.
Picnic by the riverside, perfectly placed,
In your presence, my worries are erased.

This moment, this memory, marvelously made,
Your laughter the light in the riverside shade.
With you, my love, life's never bland,
On any afternoon, by your hand.

The Kiss

Under the sudden spring shower's surprise,
Your lips press to mine, a perfect prize.
The rain rinses the world, renders it new,
But all that exists is me and you.

The droplets drum down, a delicate dance,
Blurring the boundaries by sweet chance.
Your kiss, a cocoon in the chaos of day,
Where worries wane and wonders stay.

Each splash a spark, a soft sonnet sung,
The wet world whispers where we are flung.
Amid the mist, your mouth meets mine,
In this storm, a stopped, suspended time.

The press of your lips, pure and profound,
Pulses peace where passion is found.
The shower softens the scene, so sweet,
As petals on paths beneath our feet.

Rain wraps us in a rhythmic rapture,
Each drop a beat, our hearts capture.
Nature's nectar, notes of a kiss,
Nothing feels quite as full as this.

With you, the rain is a river of rhyme,
Flowing and flowering in perfect time.
In this spring shower, love's lens clear,
With your lips pressed close, the world near.

Fireside

By the flickering fire's friendly glow,
Your voice comforts as the outside winds blow.
Each word weaves through the warm night air,
Sharing stories as if secrets we declare.

In the crackling calm, your cadence clear,
Reading aloud, drawing me near.
Our favorite books become bridges, beams,
Binding us in the ballet of dreams.

The tales you tell by the fire's face,
Wrap the room in a velvet embrace.
Each syllable a soft, silken thread,
Weaving wonder around each word said.

Characters come alive, under your care,
Their voices yours, spoken so fair.
Heroes and hearts, their journeys our own,
In the flicker of flames, our fantasies shown.

The ember's glow, a golden guide,
Illuminating the love we hold inside.
As you read, the rhythm, a rhapsodic feat,
Our hearts keep time, silently beat.

Your voice, a vessel for verses to flow,
By the hearth, where no cold can grow.
In each pause, each breath you take,
The world waits, whispers in the soft fire's wake.

With every chapter, every line you read,
In the library of our love, we feed.
For in these moments, magic is spun,
Under the firelight, two hearts are one.

Waterfall

On a trail trimmed with the touch of time,
We stumbled upon a secret, sublime.
A hidden waterfall, whispering wide,
Its beauty a beacon where our hearts abide.

Your excitement erupts, eyes alight,
Discovering the dance of water and light.
The cascade's call, clear and keen,
Draws us closer to the scene serene.

In this hidden haven, just for us,
Your laughter leaps, light and luscious.
The spray splashes, sprinkles like rain,
Matching the meter of your joyful refrain.

Every droplet, a diamond in descent,
Mirrors the marvel in your eyes, content.
Around us, the forest holds its breath,
Bearing witness to a beauty, bold yet deft.

Hand in hand, hearts aligned,
In nature's niche, a treasure we find.
Your spirit soars, sings with the falls,
In every echo, your happiness calls.

This secret space, our shared delight,
Fuels our love, fires our flight.
Under the rush, the roar so grand,
I feel the press of your pulse, the pull of your hand.

Today, tomorrow, in tales to tell,
We'll remember the waterfall where wonder fell.
In the heart of the woods, with you, I see,
Every discovery is a memory to be.

Waltz

Under the glow of gentle streetlights,
You pull me close, igniting the night.
Our steps sync to the silent city's beat,
Dancing down the deserted, dreamy street.

Your laughter launches into the late air,
A melody that moves free of care.
Under orbs of old, overhead light,
We twirl and twist through the tranquil night.

The pavement pulses under our feet,
As you lead with a rhythm so sweet.
The world wanes to a whisper, just we two,
In the dance you drew, under the hue.

Streetlights cast shadows that shift and sway,
Echoing every elegant display.
Your eyes invite, ignite my own,
In every step, our love has grown.

With no music but the murmur of the town,
Our night's ballet bears its own sound.
Your hands hold hope, your smile shines,
Stealing my breath with those signs.

Surprise sings in this spontaneous spin,
Each turn under the tungsten tin.
Late night brings liberty, love's light dance,
Under the streetlights, our romance.

As we waltz the way to where we dwell,
In every gesture, my heart you spell.
In the quiet quarters of our street,
I cherish each step of your heartbeat.

Life

Together we tackle our tasks, tools in hand,
Building more than we planned, our life so grand.
From furniture frames to foundations of dreams,
Every moment melds into shared schemes.

Your laughter lifts me, light and free,
As we piece together our shared reality.
Sawdust scatters, a sign of our toil,
A testament to our love and loyal.

Screws and sentiments securely set,
In wood and in word, our future's bet.
Your eyes alight with a brilliant belief,
In every endeavor, we find relief.

Each plank and promise precisely placed,
With the warmth of your smile, my worries erased.
Under our hands, hardwood transforms,
Into a testament of togetherness, norms.

Hammer and heart, hit in harmony,
Building beauty as we bond, you and me.
The joy of joining joint to joint,
In each task, our talents anoint.

Nails and nuances neatly aligned,
In the structure of our days, love defined.
Our workshop of wishes, where wonders don't cease,
In the sawing and sanding, we find our peace.

As we craft and create, side by side,
I cherish each chisel, each change of the tide.
In building our lives, every piece a part,
You, the frame that holds my heart.

Peace

In the soft sanctuary of our shared dawn,
Tangled together as the new day is drawn,
The morning light murmurs through the curtains' call,
Gently greeting us, tangled and small.

Your breath, a subtle song so sweet,
Synchronizes with mine, a complete
And perfect peace, as pillows share
Our dreams, draped in the dim morning air.

The warmth of your skin, woven with mine,
Crafts a cocoon, so safe, so divine.
Each ray of light that leaps and lies,
Illuminates your closed eyes, your sighs.

Under the quilt, quiet and close,
The world outside might ebb and flow,
But here in this hush, time takes its leave,
In the weave of your breath, I believe.

The soft light sifts, showing shades of you,
In this morning mosaic, made of dew.
Our limbs linked, a lattice laid,
In the light's first blush, beautifully splayed.

This tranquil tangle, this tender trap,
Where moments meld, and minutes overlap,
Here, in the harmony of our hold,
The morning's story, silently told.

Awakening with you, the world anew,
In the dawn's soft sigh, I find my cue.
To love you more, as light leaks through,
In morning's embrace, our love renews.

Festival

In the bustling heart of the festival's flair,
Your hand in mine anchors me there.
A calm in the chaos, a serene stand,
We navigate noise, hand in hand.

Around us swirls a sea of sounds,
Laughter and lyrics, the merry bounds.
Yet within this wave, a whispered peace,
In your grasp, all tumults cease.

Your fingers fold with a gentle grace,
A quiet comfort in this crowded place.
Each step assured, by your side I stay,
Guided by you through the disarray.

The lights, they flicker, flash, and flare,
A dazzling dance in the evening air.
But your eyes offer a softer glow,
A beacon I follow, the face I know.

Through the throngs, your touch remains,
A steady pulse amidst the strains.
With you, the world's rush retreats,
In your hold, my heart finds beats.

Your presence, a promise, profoundly kept,
Through each moment merrily stepped.
In this festival's frenzy, I find my rest,
With your hand in mine, feeling blessed.

As we weave through this festive throng,
Your hand in mine, I belong.
A calm island in a sea so vast,
With you, my love, securely fast.

Recount our Day

As twilight tapers, turning to the night,
We whisper words in the waning light.
Recounting our days, the dear details,
In quiet corners where comfort prevails.

Your voice, a velvet veil so soft,
Carries stories aloft.
Each sentence, a stitch in the tapestry,
Weaving our day's vast vastness snugly.

In these moments, mere murmurs mean more,
As through the day's doors we explore.
Your laughter, light, lifts the load,
Sharing secrets in our serene abode.

Under the blanket, our bed our bower,
We talk, tick by the twilight hour.
The world withdraws, its noise, its natter,
But here, your voice is all that matters.

Each detail you disclose, a delight,
Cushions our conversation through the night.
From trivial trials to triumphs true,
Each narrative nuance brings me to you.

As eyelids grow heavy, our speech slows,
Yet in the soft silence, our closeness grows.
In the hush of half-light, how I cherish,
The intimate inkling before we perish.

So let the night deepen, dark and deep,
With whispered words before we sleep.
In this quiet quest, this nightly nest,
Your presence, my peace, profoundly professed.

Wildflowers

In a field where wildflowers wildly wave,
Your fingers find mine, a feeling to save.
Gently grazing, a soft, subtle touch,
In this floral field, it means so much.

Amidst the blooms that bend and bow,
Your tender trace tells all I need to know.
Daisies dance under skies so blue,
Mirroring moments shared with you.

Your hand in mine, a silent song,
As we wander paths, where petals throng.
The sun showers us in golden light,
But none shines as bright as your eyesight.

Through lavender lanes and poppy prints,
Each step with you makes perfect sense.
The whispering winds may weave around,
Yet in your grasp, peace is profound.

Beneath the buzz of bees above,
I'm drunk on the nectar of your love.
Your caress carries the care of the day,
Sweeping the sweep of worries away.

Every brush, every touch, a bloom,
In the wildflower wonderland we consume.
With you by my side, the world's a softer place,
Each flower framed by your grace.

As we tread through this tapestry teeming,
Your love lights my life, with meaning streaming.
In this field, as your fingers find mine,
I walk in a dream, divinely designed.

Embrace

In the circle of your arms, a sanctuary found,
A fortress of feeling, where fears are unbound.
In each embrace, the world unwinds,
As peace pervades, the past behind.

Your hold, a harbor, heartening and whole,
Where warmth weaves deeply into my soul.
In the grip of your grace, griefs grow small,
Within your walls, wonders recall.

Each hug holds history, hopes, and heals,
A testament to the tenderness one feels.
Your arms arc around, an anchor in storm,
In your embrace, existence transforms.

When sorrow's shadows stretch too wide,
Your clasped comfort draws me inside.
Safety in your steadfast squeeze,
Serenity settles, unease flees.

Love's language lingers in limbs entwined,
In the press of presence, problems resigned.
Your touch, a treasure, tenderly told,
In the curl of comfort, courageously bold.

Through trials and triumphs, our togetherness tied,
In the embrace of earnest, where truth resides.
So let us linger in love's lease,
For in your arms, I find my peace.

Rose

In the garden of life, you are my rose,
Radiant and rare, where warmth enclose.
Your petals, soft and supple, speak
In colors of love, unique and sleek.

Your fragrance fills the field of days,
Guiding me through the greyest maze.
Each thorn that guards your graceful glow,
Teaches me the truths I must know.

Beneath the bud, your beauty bound,
In the soil of soul, where you are found.
With every bloom, you bring to bear,
Lessons of love, lingering there.

Morning dew mirrors your morning smile,
Capturing the charm that does beguile.
Sunshine showers, spread and spin,
In the light of your love, I begin.

With every season, you seem to show,
More of the mystery I long to know.
Your heart, a garden, generous and grand,
Where roses of our romance stand.

Even as petals may wilt and wane,
Your essence endures, remains the same.
In the winter wind or the summer's blaze,
You thrive, through the trials, in tender ways.

So here, my rose, in the garden of time,
I cherish each chapter, your rhythm and rhyme.
Forever in bloom, with colors so true,
In the garden of life, I'll always choose you.

Moonlight

Under the gentle gaze of the glowing moon,
You shine, a silvery silhouette, a serene boon.
Moonbeams meander across your skin,
Casting contours where my dreams begin.

The lunar light lands in your eyes,
A reflection of the night, clear and wise.
With each phase of the moon, you remain,
The constant in my cosmos, in your orbit, I'm fain.

You move like moonlight through mist,
Ethereal, enchanting, impossible to resist.
Each glance glows with the moon's own grace,
In the twilight, your tranquil trace.

By the brilliance of the beams that bathe you,
I find a path, precious and true.
In the silvered shadows that softly sway,
Our love lives, in layers of gray.

As stars stitch the sky, standing sentry,
Your love lights my night, a boundless entry.
In the quietude that the moonlight makes,
Your presence is the peace my heart takes.

When darkness deepens, and others wane,
Your luminescence lingers, in the lunar lane.
By moonlight, your magic, markedly felt,
In the cool calm, where my heart has dwelt.

So let us linger in this lunar light,
Where love and moon mingle in the night.
You, my moonbeam, my midnight guide,
In your light, forever I'll abide.

Serenade

Beneath the balcony, I stand to serenade,
A symphony of sounds, for you, sweetly played.
Your silhouette a shadow in the soft moonlight,
A vision so vivid on this velvet night.

With every chord that I carefully cast,
I call to our future, echo our past.
The melody weaves through the whispering wind,
In each note, a nourishment, love to commend.

You lean from the ledge, a luminous sight,
Each note I play holds us tight.
The music murmurs, a murmur mild,
Serenading you, my spirit's child.

Your smile sends shivers down the scale,
Resonating, a refrain, without fail.
Our song soars into the starlit sky,
Carried on chords that climb so high.

In the serenade, our souls entwine,
With harmonies that hint at the divine.
Your laughter lilts through the lustrous air,
Answering my anthem with grace so fair.

My guitar gently strums the strings of the heart,
In every melody, you are a part.
Under your window, I vow anew,
Through tunes and time, I'll always choose you.

So stay at your window while I play below,
Let our love's serenade sweetly grow.
In each verse, a promise, in each chorus, care,
In our love's serenade, a life we share.

Starlight

Beneath the blanket of beckoning starlight,
Your eyes echo the evening's bright.
Stars spill secrets in their silent song,
Guiding us gently, where hearts belong.

Your laughter lingers like lines of light,
Tracing trajectories through the night.
Each giggle a glimmer, a gracious glow,
In the celestial sea, our feelings flow.

Starlit strolls, our steps align,
Under the universe, your hand in mine.
Every whisper woven in the wind,
Is star-kissed, significant, intertwined.

In the cool clarity of cosmic view,
I find the universe reflected in you.
Your soul, a spectrum, sparkles so vast,
Amidst the astral, our anchor is cast.

The constellations can't compare,
To the radiance your presence wears.
Each star a story, a stellar trace,
But none as profound as your face.

Amid these orbs that overhead roam,
Your love, a light leading me home.
Through twilight's tapestry, tender and true,
In starlight, my sky finds its hue.

So let the stars in their endless grace,
Lend us their luster in this embrace.
For under this expansive, eternal dome,
In your starlit smile, I have found my home.

Gaze

In the depth of your gaze, a galaxy spins,
Stars and secrets held within.
Your eyes, the entrance to empires unseen,
Echoes of everything you've been.

They hold the hush of hidden realms,
Commanders calm at their helms.
In your look, a language lies,
Soft stories sung beneath your skies.

Gazing into your gracious gaze,
I wander within your wistful ways.
Every glance gives a golden glow,
Guiding me to the grace you show.

Your eyes, enigmas wrapped in rays,
Reveal the roads of our shared days.
In them, the texture of time is told,
A tapestry, tender and bold.

In the silence of our stare,
Speech is superfluous there.
Your pupils pull me past the plain,
Into the depth of your domain.

With every blink, beauty anew,
A cascade of clues, a view to pursue.
Your gaze, a gateway, grand and wide,
Where I wander, wish, and hide.

So let me linger longer still,
Lost in the look that loves and fills.
In the gaze that grants me ground,
I've found the love that's truly profound.

Heartbeat

In the rhythm of your heartbeat's gentle drum,
I find a melody, where love is from.
Your pulse, a pattern, perfect and pure,
A song that sings of a love so sure.

Each beat a blessing, a beautiful bind,
Connecting hearts, with every find.
Your heart's hush hums, a harmonious sound,
In its echo, endless love is found.

Through silent nights and days so bright,
Your heartbeat holds me, warm and tight.
Its cadence, a comfort, calm and clear,
Guiding me gently, always near.

With every throb, your love's embrace,
A tender touch, a tranquil trace.
In the lull of your loving beat,
I find my world, my safe retreat.

Your heartbeat whispers in softest tones,
A symphony where our love has grown.
In its rhythm, a radiant rhyme,
Marking moments, mending time.

Beneath my ear, your heart declares,
A love that lingers, lives, and cares.
Its steady sound, a sacred song,
In its music, I belong.

So let your heart keep beating true,
In every pulse, my love renew.
For in the sound of your heart's grace,
I've found my home, my perfect place.

Twilight

In twilight's tender, tranquil touch,
Your silhouette stands, soft and such.
The fading light frames your form,
As evening enters, quiet and warm.

The sky shifts, shedding its blue,
Adopting hues of a darker hue.
Your eyes, in the dimming light, still gleam,
Holding the day's last golden beam.

Twilight tints everything in sight,
But none more lovely than you tonight.
Your presence paints the perfect end,
To every day, my love, my friend.

The horizon hugs the sun's last sigh,
While stars start whispering in the sky.
Beneath this spectacle so vast,
I hold your hand, as shadows cast.

In these moments, as night takes its cue,
The world quiets, leaving just us two.
Your whisper winds through the cooling air,
A melody mild, beyond compare.

As dusk deepens, drawing its veil,
Your love, the light that does not fail.
In twilight's embrace, we find our peace,
In your arms, all searches cease.

So let twilight trace our time together,
In gentle grays, no matter the weather.
For in its grasp, grace unfolds,
In your love, my heart holds.

Passion

In the fervor of our fireside chats,
Your passion pulses, and there it sits.
It dances in your deep-set eyes,
Blazing like the bonfire skies.

Each word you whisper, warmly wrapped,
In layers of love, tightly trapped.
Your touch, a tempest, tender, true,
Stirs the stillness in the dew.

Your laughter leaps through layers of air,
Igniting sparks everywhere.
With every kiss, a kindled flame,
A burning bright that speaks your name.

The heat of your heart, held so near,
Melts away each frozen fear.
Your spirit soars, a skyward flight,
Fueling the furnace of the night.

In the dance of our daring dreams,
Your passion paints in prismatic beams.
A fervent force, so fierce and free,
In its embrace, I long to be.

Your energy erupts, a vibrant verse,
In the rhythm of the universe.
A fervor that fills the quiet space,
With a radiant, resounding grace.

So let us love, let passion lead,
In every thought, in every deed.
For in the fire of your fierce glow,
I find a love that never grows cold.

Dream

In the dreamscape of our dusk-drawn days,
You glide through my sleep in a gentle haze.
A vision vivid in the veil of night,
Where stars stitch scenes with soft-spun light.

In every dream, you dawn so dear,
A whispering wind that feels so near.
Your touch, a trace in the tranquil air,
Drawing me deeper into your care.

The night unfolds like a narrative new,
Each scene suffused with the essence of you.
In dreams, your dance delicately turns,
In the theater of sleep, where longing burns.

Your laughter lingers in lunar beams,
A melody woven through my wandering dreams.
Each glance a gem in the garden of night,
Glowing graciously under the moon's light.

Your love, a lantern in the labyrinth of sleep,
Guiding me gently through the slumber so deep.
Every whisper a wave in the wistful sea,
Carrying currents that bring you to me.

Awake, I wonder, was it all a dream?
The softness of your smile, a mere moonbeam?
Yet beside me, you breathe, real and serene,
Blurring the bounds between seen and unseen.

In the hush of dawn, your hand finds mine,
Proof that love, like dreams, does not confine.
In the waking world or in dreams' embrace,
With you, every reality I wish to face.

Enchantment

In the enchantment of each evening's end,
Your presence proves my perfect amends.
As shadows stretch and stars appear,
Magic murmurs when you are near.

Under the umbrage of an ancient oak,
Your laughter lifts, no need to provoke.
Enchanted evenings, when you're in sight,
Turn mundane moments into delight.

Each gesture graced with genteel glow,
Captivates more than you could know.
Your eyes, emerald pools profound,
In their depths, my dreams are found.

Whispered words weave through the air,
Spells of sweetness, none compare.
Your touch, a talisman so true,
Brings blessings only known to few.

With you, the world wears a wondrous face,
Full of wonder, wrapped in grace.
A sorceress of simple joys,
Commanding calm with the quietest voice.

The enchantment envelops, ever so tight,
In the lattice of love's light.
Each day dawns with a deeper spell,
In your arms, all fears quell.

So continue to conjure your gentle charms,
For I am happiest held in your arms.
In the magic of your mere presence,
I find my heart's quintessence.

The Caress

In the quiet curve of evening's caress,
Your touch whispers through my stress.
A gentle gesture, graced with grace,
In your embrace, my fears erase.

Your fingers flit with feather's touch,
Transforming moments, meaning much.
The softness of your hands, so sweet,
Brings balance where our burdens meet.

As sunlight slips into the night,
Your caress carries calming light.
Under stars that script the skies,
I find solace in your sighs.

Each stroke speaks volumes, soft and slow,
In the language only lovers know.
Your palm's path, a painted prose,
Soothes my spirit, repose bestows.

Beneath your hands, a haven formed,
Where heartaches heal, and hopes are warmed.
The world withdraws, its noise, its natter,
But in your touch, only us matters.

In the tender tracing of your trace,
Time holds tender, a gentle pace.
A comfort comes, not coy or crass,
In the quiet cradle of your caress.

So let your love, in layers light,
Lay upon me through the night.
For in each touch, your tenderness,
Grants a grace that gods might bless.

The Firefly

In twilight's tapestry, you twinkle like a firefly,
Flashing forth in the fading sky.
Your light, a luminescent lure,
Guides me gently, its glow so pure.

Around you, the air adopts a gentle gleam,
Echoing each ephemeral dream.
As fireflies flit through fields at night,
Your spirit soars, a sight so bright.

With every pulse, a pattern shows,
In the dance where deep darkness glows.
Your laughter, a light in the layered dusk,
Cuts through the shadows, a dawn from dust.

You spark against the sprawling dark,
A beacon where hope's marks embark.
Each flash, a fleeting, flickering flame,
Spells out the syllables of your name.

In this night, as fireflies play,
Your love lights paths, paves the way.
Amid the mystery of their silent flicker,
Your heart's beat, to mine, grows quicker.

Like a firefly caught in a summer's jar,
Your brilliance beckons, near and far.
But unlike those caught, you'll always be
The light that flies, forever free.

So let us wander where fireflies roam,
Under stars in the sky's high dome.
For in your glow, I find my way,
By your light, I'll always stay.

The Glance

In the fleeting flicker of a glance,
I find the fabric of our romance.
Your eyes, the embers of evening's light,
Hold the history of our hearts tight.

Each look, a labyrinth where I lose my way,
Captured in the cosmos of your gaze.
The subtle shimmer of your sight,
Illuminates the ink of night.

In the quick quiet of a passing peek,
Whispered words we need not speak.
Your gaze, a gateway to your soul,
Draws me deeper, makes me whole.

Within your glance, galaxies unfold,
Stories of the stars, silently told.
Your eyes, averse to the mundane,
Mirror the mystery of moonlit rain.

With every glance, you grant me grace,
In the simple sanctuary of your face.
A single look, a silent sonnet,
In the currency of glance, you're opulent.

When you glance, the world grows still,
Paused in the power of your will.
Through the portal of your piercing look,
I read you like an open book.

Your gaze, a guide through the grays,
In the glance game, where love plays.
So here I stand, held in your sight,
In the glance you give, my guiding light.

Velvet

In the velvet vault of our shared nights,
Your touch, a tapestry, takes to new heights.
Soft as the silk of the darkest hue,
Your whispers wrap warmth in shades so true.

Your laughter lingers, a lush, rich sound,
Like velvet vibrations profound.
Each word you weave, a wondrous gift,
Lifts my spirits, sets them adrift.

Your skin against mine, smooth and fine,
Feels like the finest velvet divine.
In every embrace, I sense the brush,
Of a velvet veil, in the quiet hush.

The curve of your cheek, under my lips,
Soft as the velvet of night's eclipse.
In your presence, my heart finds repose,
As gentle and sure as a velvet rose.

The depth of your eyes, dark and deep,
Hold me like velvet, sweet secrets keep.
In their gaze, a comforting fold,
A treasure trove of stories untold.

Your love, like velvet, rich and rare,
Envelops me in a soft, lush lair.
Every moment with you, exquisitely felt,
In the luxury of love, like velvet melt.

So let us continue, hand in hand,
Wrapped in the velvet of this love so grand.
In the texture of your tender care,
I find a velvet solace rare.

Beach Fire

By the beach bonfire's blazing bright,
Your eyes sparkle, stealing the night.
Marshmallows melt in our merry hands,
As stars above make their subtle stands.

Your laughter lights the twilight air,
Glowing with a grace beyond compare.
Each flicker, a flame in your gaze,
Outshines the stars with its radiant rays.

The bonfire burns, a beacon bold,
Yet your eyes are where my dreams unfold.
The stars grow jealous, their light fades,
In the brilliance your glance cascades.

With every crackle, every spark,
Your eyes reflect the fire's mark.
Their shimmer sings a soft, sweet song,
A melody where my heart belongs.

In this tender, toasty, twilight time,
Your eyes, the focus of my rhyme.
The bonfire blazes, but can't compete,
With the glow that makes my world complete.

As marshmallows toast to a golden hue,
I'm lost in the luminosity of you.
The stars may scatter in the sky,
But they can't match your sparkle high.

Here by the bonfire's warming wave,
Your eyes, the light that loves and saves.
In their depths, I see the glow,
That makes the stars' own envy show.

So let the fire flicker, flames ascend,
With you, my love, my light, my friend.
In your eyes, the world is right,
Sparkling with love, all through the night.

Under the Oak

In sudden showers, we dash and dart,
Our laughter echoes, lightens the heart.
Through the downpour, drenched and free,
We find shelter beneath an old oak tree.

Your smile shines through the rainy haze,
A beacon bright in the stormy maze.
Each drop dances on leaves above,
But here with you, I feel pure love.

The oak's embrace, broad and bold,
Keeps us warm from the wet and cold.
Our laughter lingers, light and loud,
An echo in the stormy shroud.

Your hair, soaked, clings to your face,
Yet your beauty blooms in this wild place.
With every laugh, a joyous sound,
In the rain's rhythm, our hearts are found.

The rain's refrain, a soothing song,
In your arms, where I belong.
Under the oak's ancient, arching arms,
I find solace in your charms.

Raindrops race down the bark's rough line,
In this moment, you are mine.
Our laughter lifts, a lively tune,
Dancing under the silver moon.

The storm may roar, the skies may weep,
But in your gaze, my soul finds sleep.
In the echo of our laughter's light,
We turn the tempest into delight.

So let the rain rage, let it pour,
For in your love, I want no more.
Under the oak, with you, my dear,
Every storm fades, every fear.

A Stolen Kiss

Behind the waterfall, where waters roar,
We find a world that's ours and more.
A stolen kiss, in the secret shade,
Where love's echoes never fade.

The cascade crashes, a curtain clear,
Muffling the world's distant cheer.
In this hidden haven, hearts collide,
With only the sound of the rushing tide.

Your lips, like whispers, soft and sweet,
Meet mine in a moment, tender, complete.
The water's whisper, a wild embrace,
Hides our love in this hidden place.

Spray and sparkle dance in the air,
As we stand together, without a care.
In the waterfall's wake, worries wane,
Leaving only love's sweet refrain.

Each drop that drips, a delicate beat,
Matches the rhythm of hearts that meet.
The world fades away, its worries washed,
In this liquid lullaby, love embossed.

With every kiss, a promise made,
In the waterfall's wonder, our love displayed.
Your touch, a treasure, tender and true,
In the misty magic, I'm lost in you.

The roar of the water, a sacred sound,
Encircles us, a love unbound.
In the cascade's caress, our secrets keep,
A stolen kiss, where the world sleeps.

So let the waters endlessly flow,
For in this place, our love will grow.
Behind the waterfall, wild and free,
Only you and I, eternally.

Breathe

In the crisp winter air, our breaths combine,
Sharing warmth from a single scarf, entwined.
Your smile sparkles in the frosty light,
A beacon bright in the cold, clear night.

Our breaths, like whispers, weave and wind,
In the icy air, love's warmth we find.
The scarf snugly wraps, our haven, our hold,
Binding us close in the winter's bold.

Your laughter lingers, light and free,
A melody that melts the freeze.
In the scarf's soft embrace, we stay,
Defying the chill of the winter's day.

Cheeks kissed by the cold's tender bite,
Your eyes gleam with a gentle light.
Our breaths blend in a misty dance,
A tender touch in the night's expanse.

With every step, snow softly sways,
Under the moon's mellow rays.
The scarf shelters, keeps us near,
Guarding our love against winter's fear.

Your hand in mine, a perfect fit,
In the stillness of the snowy quiet.
Each breath a promise, pure and true,
In the winter's wonder, I'm wrapped in you.

So let the winter winds weave and wail,
In our shared warmth, we shall prevail.
For in this scarf, in your sweet sighs,
I find my heaven, where love never dies.

The Note

In the quiet of the afternoon's embrace,
You find a note hidden in your book's space.
A surprise, a secret, sweet and small,
A love letter that makes your heart enthrall.

As pages part, my words appear,
Written with love, tender and clear.
Your smile sparkles, eyes softly gleam,
In this moment, a shared dream.

Each line laced with affection's art,
Crafted carefully to touch your heart.
In the silence, as you softly read,
My love for you, in every word, is freed.

Your fingers trace the tender text,
Each sentiment a heart's context.
A hidden message, heartfelt and true,
Meant to whisper, "I love you."

The quiet room, a sacred space,
Holds the magic of this moment's grace.
Your heart leaps, a joyous beat,
As my words and your world sweetly meet.

In the margins of your book's embrace,
My love note finds its cherished place.
A secret shared, a bond renewed,
In the quiet, our love is viewed.

As you read, a tender tear,
Falls gently, reflecting cheer.
In this simple, sweet surprise,
Our love shines, never disguised.

So keep my note within your book,
A hidden treasure, take a look.
For every word, in ink and thought,
Is a piece of the love we've sought.

The Boat

On a moonlit lake, we gently glide,
In the boat's soft sway, side by side.
Your smile, a beacon, bright and bold,
In the night's embrace, pure love unfolds.

The water whispers, waves so slight,
Reflecting the moon's tender light.
Your laughter lingers, light and free,
A melody that moves with the sea.

Stars above, their silent songs sing,
In the boat's sway, our hearts take wing.
Your hand in mine, a cherished clasp,
In the tranquil night, our moments grasp.

Each ripple dances, a gentle tease,
Echoing the night's soothing breeze.
In the boat's embrace, just us two,
The world fades, leaving me and you.

Your eyes, like stars, softly gleam,
In this serene, silvery dream.
The lake's lullaby, a whispered tune,
Carries our love beneath the moon.

In the boat's sway, our souls unite,
Beneath the canopy of endless night.
Your touch, a tender, warm caress,
In this moment, pure happiness.

As we drift in the moonlit glow,
Our love's depth begins to show.
With every sway, with every sigh,
In your presence, I touch the sky.

So let the boat and night be kind,
In this serene space, our hearts aligned.
For in the gentle sway, I see,
A love that's bound eternally.

Cafe

In a bustling café's quiet corner,
We find our refuge, time turns warmer.
Our hands touch softly, fingers entwined,
In whispered words, our hearts aligned.

Your smile, a sunbeam, bright and bold,
Warms the moment, stories told.
Small talk weaves through the clinking cups,
While love's deep silence slowly erupts.

The aroma of coffee, rich and sweet,
Wraps around us, a comforting sheet.
Your laughter lingers, light and free,
A melody that means so much to me.

In this haven, hidden from the crowd,
Our world whispers, never loud.
Your eyes, they sparkle, clear and bright,
Holding my gaze in tender light.

Every gesture, gentle and kind,
In this café's corner, peace we find.
The bustling world, a distant hum,
In your presence, I feel home.

With each sip, we share our dreams,
In this café's corner, love redeems.
Your touch, a tender tethered line,
Binding us in this moment divine.

As time ticks by, unnoticed, sweet,
In this small space, our souls meet.
The noise around us fades away,
Leaving just us in love's array.

So let the café clatter on,
In this quiet corner, we belong.
For in your touch, your gentle grace,
I've found my home, my sacred space.

Steam

In the steamy haze of our bathroom's glow,
A secret message, love's silent show.
Your name I write with careful, kind care,
In foggy letters, a love laid bare.

Your laughter lingers, light and low,
As the mirror's mist begins to show.
Each word I write, a whispered plea,
A tender touch for you to see.

The steam surrounds, a soft, warm veil,
Where love's sweet secrets never fail.
Your eyes meet mine, in soft surprise,
In the steamy script, our love lies.

The mirror captures our fleeting fun,
In fog and warmth, where two are one.
Your touch erases, but love remains,
In every stroke, my heart explains.

Messages hidden in the morning mist,
Each letter lingers, a gentle twist.
In the bathroom's quiet, calm embrace,
I see the joy upon your face.

Our secret script, so simple, sweet,
In the steamy mirror, our love's complete.
Every morning brings a chance to write,
A message of love in the soft, warm light.

With each new day, the steam will rise,
And in its haze, my love complies.
Your name, a mantra, a melody,
Written in warmth, for you to see.

So let the steam and love combine,
In secret messages, line by line.
For in this foggy, fleeting art,
I leave a piece of my loving heart.

The Cinema

In the cinema's soft, shadowy glow,
Your hand brushes mine, a spark does show.
An electric touch, a silent thrill,
In the darkened room, time stands still.

Your fingers flit, a feathered caress,
Sending shivers through, I must confess.
The screen's bright story fades away,
As your touch turns night into day.

In the hush of the hall, hearts align,
With a simple, soft, electric sign.
Your hand's warm whisper, light and free,
Speaks volumes in its silent plea.

A moment fleeting, yet so profound,
In the cinema's calm, a love unbound.
Your touch, a tether, tender and true,
Ignites a fire, as embers do.

Every accidental brush, a clue,
Of the deep connection shared by two.
Your hand in mine, a hidden dance,
A stolen second, a sweet romance.

As the movie plays its part on screen,
Our love story unfolds, unseen.
In the quiet corner of this space,
Your touch transforms, a tender trace.

Electric currents, softly flow,
From your hand to mine, a gentle glow.
In the cinema's spell, dark and deep,
Our hands hold secrets that we keep.

So let the film continue on,
While in this touch, our love is drawn.
In the shadowed seats, hearts beat as one,
An electric touch, our love begun.

The Frig

In the quiet calm of midnight's embrace,
We sneak to the kitchen, light on our face.
A late-night raid, a snack shared in glee,
With giggles and secrets, just you and me.

The fridge light glows, a gentle gleam,
Illuminating our impromptu dream.
Your laughter lilts, a lovely sound,
In this stolen moment, joy is found.

Hands reach for treats, fingers entwine,
A whispered joke, your eyes align.
The world asleep, but we are awake,
In the soft, silent joy we make.

Cheese and crackers, a midnight feast,
In your smile, my worries ceased.
The fridge's glow, our guiding light,
In the heart of the hushed, happy night.

Your voice, a melody, soft and sweet,
In this secret, secluded retreat.
Each word you whisper, warms my heart,
In the glow of the fridge, love's work of art.

Together we stand, in this quiet hour,
Our bond grows stronger, a blooming flower.
With every giggle, every shared bite,
Our love shines brighter in the fridge's light.

So let the night be our secret space,
Where laughter and love leave their trace.
In the kitchen's calm, we find our way,
Sharing snacks and secrets till the break of day.

For in these moments, small and bright,
We weave our love in the soft fridge light.
And every night, when the world is still,
I'll treasure these times, our love's sweet thrill.

The Tree

In our backyard, where dreams take root,
We plant a tree, a promise to suit.
With careful hands, we dig and place,
A symbol of love, in this sacred space.

The soil, so soft, our fingers mold,
Nurturing hope in the earth's gentle hold.
Your laughter lingers, light and free,
As we plant our future, in this tree.

Each shovel stroke, a silent vow,
To love and cherish, here and now.
With tender touch, we press the ground,
In this quiet act, our love is found.

Years will pass, and seasons change,
Yet this tree will grow within our range.
Its branches broad, its roots run deep,
A testament to the promises we keep.

We'll come back here, hand in hand,
To see the tree, so tall and grand.
Its shade will shelter, leaves will dance,
A living symbol of our romance.

In spring's sweet bloom, or autumn's gold,
Our tree will tell the tales we've told.
Through summer's heat and winter's chill,
Its growth reflects our steadfast will.

So let this tree, in years to come,
Remind us of where we've begun.
For in its growth, our love will see,
The strength and beauty of you and me.

Together we'll watch its branches spread,
A living testament to words unsaid.
And in its shade, we'll find our rest,
Knowing our love has truly blessed.

The Wishing Well

By the wishing well, where waters dwell,
We toss our coins, casting dreams to tell.
Each coin a hope, each wish a prayer,
In the quiet air, our love laid bare.

Whispered wishes, soft and sweet,
In the well's depth, our secrets meet.
Your eyes reflect the moon's soft glow,
In this sacred space, our hearts overflow.

With every coin that breaks the surface,
Our whispered hopes, in love's service.
Your hand in mine, a tender tether,
In this moment, we are bound forever.

The water's whisper, a gentle song,
Carries our dreams all night long.
In the well's depths, our desires deep,
Promises we make, forever to keep.

Our wishes float, in the twilight's grace,
Reflected in the well's tranquil face.
Your smile, a beacon, bright and clear,
Fills my heart with boundless cheer.

In the silence of the starlit night,
We share our dreams, our futures bright.
Each coin's descent, a soft, sweet sound,
In this well, our love is found.

So let us stand, in this hallowed place,
Tossing wishes with gentle grace.
For in this well, where waters swirl,
Our love is written in each ripple and curl.

Together we wish, together we dream,
In the moon's soft, silvery beam.
And as our coins in the well descend,
We know our love will never end.

Tree

In our backyard, where dreams take root,
We plant a tree, our love's pursuit.
With careful hands, we dig and place,
A symbol of time, in this sacred space.

The soil so soft, our fingers mold,
Nurturing hope in the earth's gentle hold.
Your laughter lingers, light and free,
As we plant our future in this tree.

Each shovel stroke, a silent vow,
To love and cherish, here and now.
With tender touch, we press the ground,
In this quiet act, our love is found.

Years will pass, and seasons change,
Yet this tree will grow within our range.
Its branches broad, its roots run deep,
A testament to the promises we keep.

We'll come back here, hand in hand,
To see the tree, so tall and grand.
Its shade will shelter, leaves will dance,
A living symbol of our romance.

In spring's sweet bloom or autumn's gold,
Our tree will tell the tales we've told.
Through summer's heat and winter's chill,
Its growth reflects our steadfast will.

So let this tree, in years to come,
Remind us of where we've begun.
For in its growth, our love will see,
The strength and beauty of you and me.

Together we'll watch its branches spread,
A living testament to words unsaid.
And in its shade, we'll find our rest,
Knowing our love is truly blessed.

Now you have everything you need to better deal with romantic love poems, it's time to pass on your new found knowledge and show other readers where they can find the same help.

Simply by leaving your favorable opinion of this book on Amazon, you'll show other readers where they can find the love poetry they're looking for.

Thank you for your help.   Helping readers find excellent romantic love poetry is kept alive when we pass on our knowledge – and you're helping me to do just that.

Just leave your review on Amazon or Audible.

Made in the USA
Monee, IL
15 December 2024

823c7014-88df-4e1f-b405-c1049bee518aR01